PIONEERS

Volume 11

Tales of the Wild West Series

Rick Steber

Illustrations by Don Gray

NOTE
Pioneers is the eleventh book in the
Tales of the Wild West Series

Pioneers
Volume 11
Tales of the Wild West Series

All rights reserved.
Copyright © 1993 by Rick Steber
Illustrations Copyright © 1993 by Don Gray
ISBN 0-945134-11-8

Bonanza Publishing
Box 204
Prineville, Oregon 97754

INTRODUCTION

Mountain men and fur traders were the first to travel the route that would one day become the Oregon Trail. In their wake came missionaries who wrote letters and reports describing the far side of the continent and praising the mild climate, healthful conditions and the deep, fertile soil.

Historians recognize 1843 as the official beginning of the Oregon Trail. That spring a group of a thousand land-hungry pioneers with 120 wagons and 5,000 head of cattle departed from Elm Grove, Missouri. Some of their wagons were abandoned along the Snake plateau but other were brought to the Columbia River where flat-bottomed boats were built and floated through the dangerous rapids of the Columbia Gorge to the Willamette Valley.

It took the pioneers from early spring until late fall to reach the far west. They threw together shelters and subsisted that first winter on fish, game and the generosity of their neighbors, both white and Indian. Come spring they cleared ground, tilled the virgin soil and planted crops.

The heyday of the Oregon Trail occurred after gold was discovered in California in 1848; it is estimated one-quarter million pioneers traveled overland on the Oregon Trail. From these early emigrants the social fabric of the West was woven.

Within a few years communities were established and schools and churches were built. Then came stage lines, mail deliveries, railroads, telegraph wires and the other trappings of the white man's civilization.

THE CROSSING

"I tell you it was nearly as difficult reaching the west side of the Missouri River, the jumping off spot for the Oregon Trail, as was the entire two thousand-mile trip from there to the Willamette Valley," related Al Hawk.

"To begin with, our journey through Indiana and Illinois was not pleasant, the weather being cold and snow plentiful. When we reached the Mississippi River we were forced to lay over in order to rest our teams. Thankfully, corn was plentiful and cheap.

"We had planned to cross the river at this point but it proved impossible due to ice. We had to wait for warmer weather or travel downstream, and so we headed south. Our progress was slow on account of the river being high. We were constantly having to skirt out and around marshy spots.

"Eventually a suitable crossing was located at Fort Madison. We were ferried over and immediately got under way for the Missouri River, discovering traveling across Iowa was just as bad as it could be. It was hard wheeling on account of the mud, and very tiresome walking.

"We arrived at Cainsville on the Missouri River the latter part of April and found 2,000 emigrants waiting their turn to cross. It was a terrible rush and many a squabble, from fistfights to worse, occurred.

"I passed time sitting atop an overlook, watching the ferry boats plying back and forth. The Missouri, running at near flood stage, was dangerous, being full of snags and driftwood. I witnessed several boats strike logs and go to the bottom while men and cattle struggled together in the swift current.

"On the 5th day of May, 1852, our turn came. We loaded our possessions on a flatboat and, without incident, were landed on the opposite side. Finally, our trip west over the Oregon Trail could begin."

THE PAWNEE

In 1852 Alanson Pomeroy signed on to drive an ox-drawn wagon over the Oregon Trail.

One day, not long after they crossed the Missouri River, a large band of Pawnee Indians appeared on the horizon. They wore blankets or buffalo robes around their shoulders.

Alanson was a plainsman and had experience dealing with Indians. Asked what he thought they should do he replied, "Hold council, see what they want. We pay if we have to."

One of the emigrants stated brashly, "Give 'em nothing. We have rifles. They don't have any weapons."

"Not that you see," countered Alanson, "but rest assured, they have bows and arrows and rifles and knives beneath their blankets and robes."

Suddenly the Pawnee reined in. The chief held up his hand and the captain of the wagon train rode forward to meet with him. The chief demanded payment of two cows for allowing the wagons to pass.

Payment was made. The wagons went on. But the following day the Indians appeared again with the same demand. The emigrants offered one cow, refused to pay more. The cow was led forward and this time, before the emigrants were even underway, it was killed and meat sliced off and cooked over a hastily-built fire.

Late that day, as the emigrants were making night camp, the Indians appeared a third time. They positioned themselves between the wagons and a small spring.

"That's it," said Alanson Pomeroy. "With water so near I'm not about to settle for a dry camp." He took a bucket, fearlessly marched through the line of Indians to the spring and returned with water. Following his example, other emigrants did the same. In the morning the Pawnee were gone.

DINNER INVITATION

In 1853 the Jasper family joined a wagon train bound for Oregon. One day the oxen gave out and it was decided they would lay over for a few hours, doctor the animals and travel late until they caught up to the wagon train.

That evening, as they traveled into a sun balanced on the horizon, the silhouettes of a dozen mounted Indians were observed blocking the trail. The Jaspers' wagon drew near and it was clear to see that the Indians, wearing feathers and their faces smeared with paint, were ready for war. One of them rode forward and let it be known that his party expected the Jasper family to feed them.

Andrew Jasper, the oldest of the boys, was driving the oxen. He was a hand with an ox whip and could kill a horsefly on the leader's horn or cut out the heart of a playing card at fifteen feet with just a flick of his wrist.

Andrew unlimbered the whip and in a gruff voice told the Indian, "Get out of the way. We don't plan on feeding a pack of no-account Injuns."

He started the oxen. The Indian jumped to the ground and began waving his arms to make them stop. Andrew swung the whip, it cracked with a sharp report and the Indian grabbed at his shoulder.

There was a whirl of motion; the horse rearing and pulling back, the Indian trying to mount, and again, and again, and again, and again, the black leather tip of the whip snaking out, cutting flesh. There were sharp cries of pain.

The Indian regained his mount and raced away. Andrew became aware that his mother was sobbing. He went to comfort her and told her, "It's settled."

"No, it's not! Oh, Andrew, how could you do such a thing? The Indians will come back tonight and kill us all."

Andrew replied, "I showed them what I could do with my ox whip. If they come back, I'll show them what I can do with my rifle."

4

JUMPING OFF TO OREGON

"None in my family had slept on the ground so much as a single night. But on October 5, 1850 we departed from our home in a covered wagon pulled by oxen," related John James.

"The whole village walked with us for a ways. We shook hands with aunts, uncles, cousins and friends. And then we boys scampered off down the road looking for adventure.

"That night we camped beside a stream. When I awoke everything seemed strange; the morning so fresh, so invigorating.

"We came to the Mississippi River and took passage on a boat powered with a team of horses that walked a treadmill. We landed on the Iowa side, climbed the breaks of the Mississippi and located quarters where we could winter. There was an abundance of corn in the area and Father bought fields as it stood in the shock and us boys had to go out, break off the ears, fill the wagon bed full and haul it home to feed the oxen.

"That winter we prepared ourselves for the upcoming overland trip to Oregon. It was Father's idea to manufacture everything possible within one's ability. It was difficult for Mother having to card, spin and weave cloth. We had two colors of clothes, a pale blue and a brownish brindle. Father said three suits would last me a long time; one to wear, one to get married in and one for old age.

"Father made vast quantities of hard bread. In the months to come the filling would be made as circumstances permitted, adding meat from buffalo, sage hens, jackrabbits, antelope and fish. When there was no meat the bread would be our mainstay against starvation. He also laid aside a supply of bacon and sausage. In his spare time he melted bars of lead and made bullets.

"On the 8th day of April, 1852, spring coming on, we hitched up our faithful oxen and jumped off to Oregon."

TIMES CHANGE

"I was ten years old when Father decided that the grasshoppers were making more headway in Kansas than he ever could," related May Squires. "Some of the neighbors had already given up and moved west. They had written back such glowing accounts that on the 9th day of May, in 1877, we loaded our belongings in a prairie schooner and along with a few friends departed from our home.

"Following the Oregon Trail we headed west driving mules and, since we had no feed for them, it was necessary to follow the grass. Sometimes we would be miles from the main route.

"My father always had his rifle at the ready, both for killing birds and animals and also for protection against the Indians, although we never had any trouble with Indians. I only saw him lay down his rifle one time and that was when a child died. Father made a coffin, dug the grave and covered it over with dirt. The women and children stood by the grave saying their goodbys while the men stood guard a short distance away, their rifles at the ready.

"We crossed the Blue Mountains. By then we were completely out of provisions and without money to acquire more, so we stopped. Father worked in the harvest fields and Mother and us children picked and dried fruit and berries. After a while we continued on to the Palouse country where Father located a homestead.

"I've lived all my life here and never wanted to go anywhere else. I think back sixty-odd years to when we came west, by wagon over a rocky trail, and compare it to the modern world and automobiles skimming over paved roads. The journey that took us five difficult months can now be accomplished in a matter of a few days. Times have certainly changed. They certainly have."

NEWLYWEDS

Melvina Hembree, a pioneer of 1843, recalled, "My family, the Millicans, came west by wagon and settled in the Willamette Valley. Two days after I turned 13 I married. My husband was 19 years old. When we exchanged vows I was wearing a new calico dress that Mama made me, regular store-bought shoes and even stockings.

"We took a donation land claim of 640 acres and built a cabin which we moved into at once. Within the next few days my husband made a bedstead out of fir poles, which he peeled and fastened to the wall. He pegged them together for we had no nails. On this bed we laid dried ferns for our mattress. Our table was a tree split down the middle and we had two stools. Pegs were driven into the walls for hats, coats and clothes. My only dishes were a big iron kettle, a small iron pot and an iron skillet. I had to stoop over the mud fireplace in order to cook. I baked bread in the iron skillet, pot-roasted our meat in the iron pot, baked potatoes in the ashes and browned wheat or oats for our coffee.

"My husband was a great hand to hunt. He usually turned out about daybreak and would be gone only an hour or two, returning with deer, grouse, rabbit or the like. We always had game hanging in the tree near the kitchen door.

"The first baby came along. Others followed. I took care of the babies, cooked, washed clothes, made soap and candles, knitted and darned and sewed and did all the other things that had to be done. For entertainment we used to go to preachings at the neighboring houses or to barn-raisings or house-warmings.

"The kids are grown and we have grandchildren, great-grandchildren and even a few great-great. Next year Pa and me will celebrate seven decades of being together and that's mighty good."

PIONEER HOME

"I can relate what the conditions were like in pioneer times because I crossed the plains in a covered wagon," related Mrs. Mary Stewart.

"Fortunately, before we departed I had the foresight to put a brace and bit in the wagon box. And it was a good thing I did because after we completed our journey there was not a nail in the whole Oregon country. Around the fire, while I spent my evenings making buckskin moccasins or knitting stockings, my husband whittled oak pegs.

"Our house was built from logs held together with oak pegs. The doors were split out of straight-grained wood, hand-planed and pegged together. Our floor was made of heavy timbers, roughly dressed, with the top face finished flat and of course it, too, was pegged.

"My husband split boards and made a frame for our fireplace. I hiked down to the river where I fetched clay from the clay bank in a copper kettle. I packed the clay into the wooden frame and pounded it in. The hearth, too, was made from clay and I wet and smoothed it until it was polished and flat as a chunk of iron. The chimney was of clay and sticks. We built a little fire in the fireplace and gradually baked the clay until it was the same as a solid brick.

"I did all of my cooking over this fireplace. An iron spider and a few copper kettles comprised my cooking outfit. Unless you have cooked that way you would never fully understand how tired a back can get. My one ambition in life was to someday own a stove.

"In 1851 two stoves were brought to Oregon City. I was able to secure one. Oh, what a comfort it was to be able to stand up and cook over a stove!"

THE FIRST WINTER

"We started out over the Oregon Trail in a covered wagon pulled by oxen in early April and it was not until late in October that we reached The Dalles, Oregon," recalled Elizabeth Laughlin.

"Father said it could snow at any time so, rather than trying to cross the mountains, he decided we should hole up for the winter. He began cutting trees and shaping logs for a house. He cut small trees so, with what assistance Mother could give him, he could lay them up as there was no man he could get to help him. This work was interspersed with hours in which he hunted for game to supply our table.

"Somewhere on the plains Mother had come into possession of a wagon cover made of hickory cloth. She took this cover and made shirts of it which she sold to the Indians.

"During that long winter our supplies dwindled. When we ran low on salt Father was able to buy a wet mess of rock salt out of a pork barrel for which he paid 12½ cents a pound. We ran low on flour and one day Mother announced she could not bake any more bread. That evening she made a stew of some birds Father had shot and there was just enough flour to thicken the gravy.

"About the time we were ready to sit down at the table two men, who had been down along the river hunting for lost horses, came up and asked if they could eat with us. They offered to pay $2 but Father refused their payment, told them to take a seat at the table. They ate and seemed genuinely delighted with the stew.

"After dinner the two men emptied their pockets of hardtack, which they gave to my brothers. They gave me a dollar. After they were gone I cried and cried, because I would have much preferred to have had the crackers than the money."

DECISIONS

"Well do I remember the hullabaloo set off in Fulton County, Illinois when Father announced we were headed off to Oregon!" recalled Benjamin Bonney, a pioneer of 1845.

"Neighbors tried everything to persuade Father to change his mind. They said we would starve to death, drown, get lost on the desert or be killed by Indians. Father ignored them and went about making ready for the trip. He built a box on our wagon and put in a lot of smoked and pickled pork. He made over 100 pounds of maple sugar, ground cornmeal and laid in a supply of dried meat. I remember him buying two gallons of coffee beans for a dollar and the storekeep threw in a wooden pail.

"We crossed the plains, traveled over the Rocky Mountains at South Pass. Our trip was uneventful until we reached Fort Hall on the Snake River. Here we were met by a picturesque old man by the name of Caleb Greenwood. He was dressed in buckskins, had a long beard and told us the road to Oregon was dangerous on account of the Indians. Then he offered to lead us to California, saying he represented Captain Sutter and promising all who followed him would receive potatoes, coffee and dried beef. He further promised that when they reached California each man would be given six sections of land from Sutter's Spanish land grant.

"That night around the campfire the men discussed the matter. Those against it said no red-blooded American should want to go to a land under Spanish rule and that the land titles in California were uncertain. In the morning my father swung our wagon out of the line and eight others followed. We were on our way to California.

"As we pulled away one of the men going on to Oregon called out to us, 'Your bones will either whiten in the desert or be gnawed on by wild animals in the mountains. Goodby! We will never see you again.'"

11

GOOD SAVER

"Growing up in the West, I learned the real value of money," related F.E. Settlemier.

"I bucked straw at one dollar a day, working from sun-up until dark. I will never forget how rich I felt when I came home with my first week's wages — six big silver dollars. I was afraid I would be held up on the way home so I ran most of the way. Once I got home I began worrying for fear a burglar would take my money, so I buried it. Then I began to worry for fear someone would find the hiding place, so I dug it up and divided it in three parts and buried two dollars in each of the three different hiding places.

"When I was a kid, back in the late 1860s, Father hired some Chinamen to dig potatoes. I had been working hard and he had promised me I could go to the state fair. But the Chinamen were not very careful workers and as a result quite a few spuds remained in the field. My father was a man slow to give his word but he always kept it. He said to me, 'I know I promised you could go to the state fair today. But if you will give up your trip and harrow the potato field, I will walk behind and pick up potatoes. We will split whatever we get.' I gave up my trip and we managed a wagon load of potatoes which Father sold for $12.

"Another of my money-making enterprises involved my appetite for cherries. I saved the pits, planted them, took care of the seedlings and sold them to Father. With this money I bought a Jersey bull which I eventually sold for $100. This money I invested in horses. One day a freight train killed two of my horses and broke the jaw and dislocated the shoulder on another. The railroad claim agent allowed me $75 apiece for my three horses. But the one that was injured was far from dead. He lived to be 28 years old and was one of the best horses I ever drove.

"As a kid I was not only a good worker but also a good saver. The day I turned 18 I had $1,700 in the bank."

LIFE IN THE BACK COUNTRY

Alexander Brender came west in 1880 and filed on a homestead in a secluded valley in the northern Cascade Mountains. He related, "I built a log cabin, cut wild hay and planted a garden. Month in, month out I would see no one but an occasional passing Indian. They were always welcome guests.

"Every few months I would come down to the trading post and receive my mail. My contact with the outside was through newspapers. I subscribed to the San Francisco *Chronicle*, the Denver *Rocky Mountain News*, the New York *World* and a Chicago paper, the name of which escapes me. I would take the bundle of newspapers up to my cabin and read every word. I probably knew more about the world than people in the cities did.

"For six long years I bached and wrestled with the skillet and sourdough. And then a friend of mine wrote to a widow woman about a thrifty bachelor who lived in a valley way back in the mountains. To make a long story short, an introduction was arranged. I met Mrs. Samantha Trout, bounced her three youngsters on my lap, and within a short time we agreed on matrimony.

"Samantha was from Mississippi and she learned in a hurry that out west we lived by our own efforts, on the food we raised and the things we could fashion with our own two hands. A box nailed to a log was a cupboard. A bunk was a bed. She cooked in a fireplace. The furniture, made of split pine, sufficed. And as time passed the homestead took on the air of an estate. Seasons and crops and babies filled her time.

"In addition to her three youngsters Samantha gave me four sons of my own. They are grown and married. I have 12 grandchildren. They all live here on the original homestead. This place that I settled shall always be known as Brender Valley."

FATHER AND SON

The spring of 1865 a wagon train bound for Oregon pulled out of Missouri. Among the pioneers was a Baptist preacher and his family. The pioneers had been warned of the dangers from roving bands of Indians as well as from bushwhackers, leftovers from the Civil War. Each night guards were posted.

There came a night when the preacher was assigned the second guard shift, replacing his son. Late that night he crawled from bed, stepped down from the wagon, wrapped a blanket around his shoulders, picked up his rifle and headed toward the little bluff where his son was standing guard.

The son had been listening to coyotes and was edgy. Out of the corner of his eye he caught movement but just then the moon slid behind a cloud and a curtain of darkness was pulled over the land. He waited and finally the moon reappeared and he could see more than movement. There was a figure, a man.

The butt of the young man's rifle was tight against his shoulder. Index finger curled against the trigger. And then fire belched from the end of the barrel. The figure pitched forward onto the ground. Booming thunder roared, bounced between the hills, echoing and re-echoing.

The young man, voice high-pitched and excited, yelled, "That's one Indian that'll steal no more stock!"

The young man and pioneers from the wagon train converged on the lifeless figure. The blanket was pulled back. When the son realized he had killed his father he let out a hair-raising scream of anguish.

The minister was buried between the wheel ruts of the Oregon Trail. Ashes from the campfire were scattered over his grave and the cattle were driven over it to conceal it from grave robbers. The wagon train continued west.

GROWING UP

"When I was young, kids of my day and age had to be responsible and useful around the home and in the fields," stated Marilla Bailey.

"I was married at age 15 and not only was I an accomplished cook and housekeeper, but I knew how to take care of babies from having cared for my brothers and sister. I could paddle my canoe as well as an Indian. And I was an accomplished hand with horses.

"My husband was a logger and gone a good deal of the time. I rustled the living for myself and the children. We lived largely on game. I could handle a revolver or a rifle; used to shoot deer, elk, bear, and could pop the heads off grouse and pheasants with a six-shooter. In fact, I became so expert with a revolver I could out-shoot nine out of ten men.

"Occasionally I would go out in the woods with my husband. We lived in tents, log cabins and sometimes in log pens. But then my husband died, leaving me with ten children to raise. I moved to town, took in boarders and operated a rooming house.

"The modern mother would think twice before she would allow her 15-year-old daughter to get married and move out into the timber, miles away from any other settlers, kill game to eat, cook over a fireplace, make soap and candles and clothes, take care of her children, nurse them when they were sick and live alone for weeks at a time.

"I was an Oregon Trail pioneer, coming west with my family in 1852. Seventy-four years have passed since then and the most noticeable change I see is in how much more is done for the girls of today than was done for girls of my generation. Today's girl has liberties that I would never have dreamed of. But I just have to wonder if they are as self-reliant, self-sacrificing and as useful as we had to be when I was young. I think not."

MEASLES

Pioneer Martha Collins related a memory from her childhood. "It was us wagon emigrants who brought the measles to Oregon. The Indians did not know how to doctor it. They would go in a sweat house, then jump in a cold stream. Usually they died.

"Indian children in the camp near our cabin began dying and we could hear women wailing day and night. An Indian medicine man came to our house for protection. He said his patients all died so the Indians were going to kill him for claiming he could cure them and not doing so. When he thought the coast was clear he started off. But just then the chief, Quatley, rode up. The medicine man whipped his horse and tried to get away. Quatley took careful aim and shot the medicine man off his horse.

"All of us children in our family had been sick with measles but we recovered. Quatley said to Mother, 'Your children live. Our children die. Your medicine stronger. My little girl sick. I want you make her well.'

"'No. I will not try. If she dies you will kill me like you killed your medicine man,' replied Mother.

"'You make her well. If she die I no blame you,' the chief told her.

"Mother had the little girl brought to our house. She kept her out of the draft and gave her herbs and teas. Soon she was well. Mother returned her to the Indian camp.

"The following morning Quatley rode up to the cabin driving a herd of horses. He told Mother, 'You save girl. Take horses.'

"'No, I could not do that. I only did what any mother would do,' she told him.

"After that Quatley kept us supplied with wild game, our loft was always full of hazelnuts and the squaws brought us all the huckleberries we could use. As long as Quatley was in the country we never lacked for food."

17

THE SAILOR

Henry Lazinka went to sea at the age of 14 and for years sailed the oceans of the world. According to him, "I loved the sea and figured to be a sailor all my days.

"And then, it was in 1883, my ship came to the Northwest and an English chap who worked with me convinced me to go with him to the Columbia plateau. He said his brother was a wealthy rancher.

"Turned out his brother was just a sheepherder, had recently lost his job and was flat broke. We stayed with him in a shack, actually there were seven of us and the total capital of all seven was less than three bucks. There were no blankets and we shared a cougar skin. Ever try to lie on the floor and make a cougar skin stretch over seven? After one night I felt the call of the sea.

"I rode a freight car to Portland only to discover my ship's papers had been sent to my friend's brother. There was a ship due to sail in two weeks for Australia. The captain said he would give me a position as third mate if I could produce my papers.

"I caught an eastbound freight. It was frightfully cold and snowed and snowed. Finally the train was forced to stop and I took off on foot. I had thirty miles to go. All I had on were light shoes and before very long they came apart. I could look over my shoulders and see red stains in my footprints on the snow.

"When finally I reached the cabin I laid on the floor and did not move for 60 hours. They rubbed coal oil over me, but in spite of that my face and feet and hands swelled up like a toy balloon. They pricked the skin and let the water run out. My skin peeled off.

"During my ordeal all I dreamed about was going back to sea. But instead of that, after I healed, I settled down in eastern Oregon and have spent the last 40-odd years ranching and farming. Never did get back to sea."

FIRE HUNT

"I'll tell this story on myself," related Northwest pioneer Ed King. "It happened the fall of 1897.

"The boys were safely tucked in bed and my wife and I were sitting in front of the fire. We discussed how good it would be to have fresh venison liver for breakfast and I decided we should go fire hunting.

"The procedure to fire hunt was for me to kneel on the floor while my wife placed a pad on my head and strapped a lantern to it using a strap under my chin and binding it like a saddle cinched on a bronco. When it was in place I could not talk or even open my mouth. But it did provide plenty of light and allowed me to keep my hands free.

"I took all the shells I could find, 13 total, and we walked to the edge of the orchard. There were several bright eyes shining at me and I took aim, fired. All at once the orchard came alive with eyes.

"I shot at eyes there, there, over there.... I missed and missed, kept right on missing until I was out of shells.

"My wife witnessed my dilemma. 'I know where there's another shell,' she said and ran to fetch the ammunition.

"She returned and I quickly loaded the shell. I took careful aim, touched it off and two bright eyes blinked out. I was positive I scored a hit. And sure enough, I discovered I had shot one of the biggest bucks ever killed in the country.

"I was a little chagrined at having killed only one deer. I had a reputation as a good shot and I didn't want the neighbors within hearing distance thinking otherwise.

"A few hours later, when it was getting light, I hitched the team to the wagon and the boys and I went to the orchard to retrieve the venison. And much to my delight we found not only the one deer but also four more dead deer. After that, my reputation intact, I breathed a little easier."

TRAIL REVISITED

"We came west in 1884," related Eva Brown. "We rented a boxcar and brought our stock, grain and household belongings to the end of the line. That was Rosebud, Montana. That was as far as the rails stretched.

"From there on we traveled by horse and covered wagons. We had three teams and wagons but even still, we had to leave many things behind and still more was left scattered along the trail. We crossed to Missoula and from there went up and over the Rocky Mountains to the Pacific Northwest.

"As far as I was concerned the worst part of the journey was that I thought I had a reasonably heavy pair of shoes but they turned out to be kid leather. Over the mountains the soles were completely gone and I walked barefoot through the snow. And over the desert I had to contend with cactus.

"In 1917 I retraced the route of our many discomforts, this time in an automobile. It was quite something. It took only a matter of days to go from Spokane Falls to Missoula. Coming out it had taken from April to July.

"There was one place on our journey where we had crossed on a ferry boat. I went directly to where we had made camp, a very nice spot, and I suppose that was why I remembered it so well: the smell of dinner, the horses nickering, a flight of geese passing overhead.

"Earlier that day we had stopped the automobile to pick strawberries. There was a farm house not far from the camp spot so I hiked over to get cream for the berries.

"Three white-haired men were living there. They remembered when the ferry operated. We talked back and forth and then I offered to pay for the cream but they refused. One of them said, 'If you crossed on that ferry in 1884 and went over that trail so long ago, you should not have to pay for cream.'

"I told him, 'If you gentlemen have lived here all those years, you should certainly be paid.' I left them a few coins."

THE PIANO

"I was engaged in partnership with my father. We had a store in the small town of Olympia, Washington where we sold toys as well as pianos and organs," told Sam Woodruff.

"In order to attract customers Father would call on me and say, 'Sam, my boy, play something.'

"One afternoon I was seated at a piano when a man wearing a broad-brimmed straw hat and coveralls tucked into work boots came strolling through the doorway.

"Father had instructed me to confine my music to rather short pieces. But when I ended the piece for the man I imagined was a farmer, he implored me, 'Play more, please.'

"And so I played. It had been my observation that most farmers enjoyed noise more than music and so I proceeded to make a lot of noise with many flourishes and runs, very little music. As I concluded, I turned to the man and inquired, 'Do you play?'

"'Yes, a little,' he answered hesitantly.

"'Come over,' I said, waving him to the piano seat, 'Sit down, give it a try. Anyone can knock out a tune on this piano.'

"He sat, raised his arms, shook back his sleeves. His fingers worked above the keyboard, playing nothing, allowing the muscles and tendons to warm themselves. And then fingertips touched ivory. My goodness! What music did they make!

"The first selection was 'Moses in Egypt' followed by several brilliantly-played classics. I was so embarrassed I would have crawled in a hole if I had found one.

"It turned out the 'farmer' was none other than Professor Nitschke, an esteemed gentleman from the East Coast. He had come west over the Oregon Trail and his party of emigrants were camped near town. In later years Professor Nitschke became world famous for his vast musical ability."

21

OREGON TRAIL BRIDE

"I was born in Missouri on March 10, 1836," related Mrs. Johnson. "Growing up I always heard a lot of talk about the Oregon Trail. Every year more folks moved west.

"There was a neighbor boy, his name was Boone Johnson, and we spent time together. Just before my 16th birthday he told me he had enlisted to drive a wagon across the plains.

"I did not much like the idea of his going so far away and my having to stay in Missouri. Although he said he would come back for me I was afraid we would never see each other again. I told him so.

"'Then we'll get married,' he said.

"We went to Father and Boone asked for my hand. But Father refused permission, said we were too young. He told Boone to go to Oregon, get himself situated and then, if he wanted to, he could come back for me.

"I did not say anything but I had a plan. See, my married sister and one of my brothers had joined the wagon train. When it pulled out I hid myself in their wagon.

"I was worried Father would come for me but he did not. After a couple of days Boone and I went to Reverend Powell and asked him to marry us. I think he was concerned about my father, too, because he said he could do nothing until after we crossed the Missouri River.

"Reverend Powell did marry us and everyone in the wagon train joined in the celebration. We had a fine dinner that included roast chicken, vegetables, bread, coffee and, best of all, we had an honest-to-goodness wedding cake.

"Our honeymoon was spent on the Oregon Trail. Boone drove the wagon for his board and I did the cooking to pay my way. It was a happy time for us."

The Johnsons reached Oregon City and wintered there. In the spring they moved out of town; Boone started a mill and built a house. They lived together in that house for a half century and during that time raised 11 children.

MEMORIES OF THE TRAIL

J.B. Wright was an old man, nearly 100 years old, when he recalled his trip over the Oregon Trail. "We pulled out of Dorris County, Iowa in April of 1863. After crossing the Missouri we had to wait a few weeks 'til the grass greened 'fore we could jump off on the Oregon Trail.

"There were other travelers, seemed like most were leaving on account of the troubled conditions caused by the Civil War. We reached Fort Kearney and were told the grass was better on the north side and so we forded the Platte River. At that point the river was a mile wide and knee-deep to an oxen, though in places it came up to the wagon bed. The bottom was sandy and you couldn't stop or else the current would wash the sand from beneath the wagon wheels.

"After crossing the Platte we found a wide and beautiful prairie of emerald green. We regularly built fires of buffalo chips and dug down through the sod a couple feet to cool, clear water. The year before there had been a drought, thousands of buffalo had perished for want of water. All along the road could be seen their bleached and whitened bones. Emigrants used the many broad shoulder blades as message boards to those who followed.

"We crossed over South Pass and I found water running west to join the Colorado River. Coming into Green River valley we met a war party of Indians, more than 400, dressed with feathers and smeared with paint. They caused us no problems but did attack a wagon train behind us, killing a man and driving off some of the stock.

"Our narrowest escape occurred near Snake River. We stopped for noon camp in a ravine. A rain came on sudden-like and we took shelter in our wagons. A few moments later a column of water, five-feet high, rolled down the gulch from the cloudburst. It swept away everything in its path. Fortunately for us, we were on a little knoll or else I wouldn't be here to tell this story."

TRIP WEST

"We took out of St. Joe, Missouri the spring of 1852," recalled Marilla Washburn. "There were 72 wagons, 8 light buggies and 170 people in our wagon train.

"Two days before we could see Chimney Rock the cholera struck us. Seven died the first night and four more the following day. I remember one young man, a very likable chap, went out to ride night guard. He was perfectly normal during supper, but within two hours after he went out he had taken the cholera and died. They brought him back to camp tied over his saddle.

"My brother and I both took sick. Mother gave us hot whiskey, internally, and she soaked flannel cloths in hot whiskey and placed them on our stomachs. We laid over a half-day but not on our account for, you see, Mother was in labor and when we once again got under way I had a new baby brother, Melvin. That made 13 children.

"Frequently we would see a cloud of dust rising and several times we barely divided our long train in time before the buffalo would come charging into view, their shaggy-haired heads held low, running at a lumbering trot toward the river. They would not stop for anything and so we gave them the right of way.

"We crossed the Rocky Mountains and the Blue Mountains and finally reached The Dalles. We piled a flatboat high with all our belongings and floated to Cascades where we portaged and took passage on a small steamer.

"By the time we reached the little settlement of Portland the winter weather had already set in and the days were gray, wet and gloomy. Mother and I wept almost as much as the rainy skies; Mother was homesick for her people and I for my schoolmates.

"Come spring Father took a homestead on the north bank of the Columbia River. We moved there. Life went on."

THE EXPRESS

"When I was a young man I never had the patience to be a homesteader. I went looking for easy money instead, chasing after gold," stated Tom Brents.

"I was with the first wave of men headed into eastern Oregon. I helped build the first cabin in the little settlement of Canyon City. It didn't take long for me to see I wasn't cut out for prospecting. Didn't have so much as an ounce of luck. But I noticed the miners were eager to send mail to loved ones and receive letters from them. Also, the Civil War was in progress and they were hungry for news from the battleground.

"I decided there was ample opportunity for me to establish a pony express route between Canyon City and the county seat, The Dalles. There were no roads in between, save for Indian trails and game trails.

"I went in with a young chap named Nelson and we organized Brents & Nelson Express. We carried the mail and brought in newspapers as well. We carried Willamette Valley papers and the Sacramento *Union*, even thought it was ten days old by the time it arrived at The Dalles. We sold all the papers we could carry and doubled our money."

The run was so profitable that before long an opposition express company was started. Naturally, the first express rider to reach Canyon City would sell all his papers while the one who came in later would have papers left on his hands and would be lucky to get his cost out of them.

Tom continued, "We began our express service with a mule and a few horses but as competition developed we were forced to upgrade our strings and establish a series of relay stations every 25 miles or so.

"The fastest run that was ever made was in June 1863. The express rider for the opposition line and myself left The Dalles together. I beat him to Canyon City, riding 225 miles in just 28 hours."

REACHING OREGON

"After crossing the continent by ox team we reached the boundary of the Oregon Territory," recalled John James. "That was in the fall of 1852.

"The valleys formed by the Burnt, Powder and Malheur rivers were attractive but the most beautiful of all was the Grande Ronde valley. This was an ideal place for emigrants to have settled but it was not considered safe from the threat posed by the various tribes of Indians who inhabited the region.

"Crossing the Blue Mountains we were met with tall pines, hemlock and some fir on the summit. We dropped to the open plain and I will never again see as many fine horses as the Cayuse Indians had managed to round up.

"The Cayuse seemed rather sullen. A few years before, after only a handful of Indians had been involved in the Whitman massacre, the Oregon Volunteers had chastised all the Cayuse. Because of such treatment the Indians were no longer friendly to the white travelers.

"Our journey across the Columbia plateau was tedious. We forded the John Day River and the next night camped on a sandbar in the Columbia River where a cold wind blew fiercely.

"The following day, coming up the hill from the Deschutes River, a group of us boys were in advance of the wagon train. We saw two men on horseback. They wore store-bought clothing and looked very clean and well-fed. The sight of them made me very aware of my holey and dirty cotton pants and shirt, no hat or shoes, and my hair all tangled and matted. I felt something moving on top of my head and brushed off a green caterpillar that, I guess, was trying to make a nest there.

"One of the men, sitting on his horse, looked me over and told the other man, 'I looked just like that boy when I came over the trail years ago.' And they rode on."

WILD ANIMALS

In his declining years P.H. Roundtree, a pioneer of 1859, used to love to sit in his rocking chair and spin stories about wild animals.

"When I first came to Oregon the grizzly bears were everywhere. Remember one time, my brother Turn and I came back from a hunting trip in the Siskiyou mountains, found a grizzly had visited my homestead, killed fourteen pigs and a hog.

"The neighbors, John Cooper and Jim Matney, joined us for the bear hunt. Had six good dogs. Started them on the bear's trail. They jumped him, stopped him within a half mile. I was on my little mare, the other boys were afoot.

"I rode to within a dozen paces, dropped the bridle reins over the saddle horn, raised my rifle to shoot. But just then the bear came out over the dogs, charged me and the mare wheeled so quick she almost lost me. She was jumping over four-foot chaparral and it was all I could do to hang on. After a couple hundred yards I managed to stop her. Coax as I might she would not go back toward the bear so I led her to a tree, tied her, proceeded on foot.

"By the time I got there Jim was taking a shot at the bear. I squeezed off the second. Turn third. John fourth. Each time the grizzly would roar and charge the puff of smoke and we would have to scamper up a tree.

"The bear finally gave up on us and limped away. We followed along and after hitting the bear 13 times more, he finally lay down and died.

"We rolled that bear up on skids and into a common wagon. His nose touched the front and his hind legs hung over the tailgate. He filled every square inch of the bed. We guessed his weight at a ton."

PERFECT AS A PICTURE

Ella and Alfred and their six children lived on a hardscrabble South Dakota homestead. Ella was pregnant with number seven.

One day, only a week from her due date, Ella left the children at home and walked the mile to the neighbor's house. She visited with her friend Greta and stayed through dinner. As the two women were washing the dishes, Greta asked, "What is wrong? Something is wrong, isn't it?"

Ella broke into tears and as she dabbed at the corners of her eyes with the drying towel, she sobbed, "Baby's comin' an' won't have a thing. No clothes, no diapers, one ol' threadbare blanket...."

"Now, now," comforted Greta. "I've got some extra material. We'll just fix you up."

Greta searched through her material pile, set aside a fifty-pound flour sack and into it placed leftover fabric from her boys' shirts, ten yards of flax and some colorful flannel.

It was getting late when Ella announced she had to be going. She was still so depressed that Greta insisted on walking her home. On the way Ella confided to her friend and neighbor, "When I came visiting I was so out of sorts that if you had not helped I might very well have ended it all."

The following day Ella's oldest girl rode to Greta's and asked, "Mama has used up all her thread. Could she borrow some?"

The baby arrived on schedule and was greeted with a generous collection of new gowns and little shirts and flannel blankets crocheted around the edges. Ella sat in the rocking chair, rocking and singing softly to the bundle in her arms. It was as perfect as a picture in a magazine.

BLIND LUCK

A group of old miners sat on a bench in front of the livery stable reminiscing about the days in the early 1850s when Jacksonville, Oregon was a boom town.

"Remember the clerk who came here from the east coast?" asked one of the miners.

"The one who went to work for Dave Birdseye?"

"That's the one," said the first man. "Beats me what possessed him to leave home and come all the way out here but I suspect jobs were scarce in the East. He told me he planned to work for a while and send for his girl. He was in love. Said she was the most beautiful girl in the whole world.

"He worked a week or two and that was all he could take. He went to Dave Birdseye and told him, 'Sir, I am terrible homesick. Could you possibly see your way clear to loan me enough for passage? I will pay you back, with interest. I promise. Please, sir.'

"Dave could be a little brusque and he was that day because, first of all, he hated to lose a clerk and second, he suspected as soon as the lad reached home he would forget his obligation.

"'I ain't a gonna loan you one red cent,' Dave told him.

"The clerk quit, ended up trying his hand at mining, staking a claim on the most unlikely ground around. We laughed at him. As a matter of fact, the joke was on us. In the span of a few days he had struck a rich pocket and washed out better than 300 ounces of nuggets and coarse gold. When the gold petered out he bought a ticket on the stage for San Francisco where he caught a ship for the East Coast. That was the last anyone around these parts ever saw or heard from him. That tenderfoot had the best case I ever did see of plain ol' blind luck."

31

INDIAN MONEY

"Having grown up in the Northwest Indian country I can give an accurate description of life among what some call 'the savages'," stated Nettie Koontz.

"When I was a child there were more Indians than white people. The stories so often related about the wickedness of the Indians are ridiculous, for they were absolutely harmless and did not steal or assault anyone.

"When we were away we never locked our doors. The only time there was trouble were those times when a bad white man sold or gave an Indian liquor. Other than those instances I would have to say the Indians were really more dependable than some of the whites.

"Once on a trip to Oregon City my father sought the services of an Indian guide. He approached the man and asked to be taken upriver. The Indian said nothing. Father tried a different course of action. He removed a coin from his pocket and, holding it so the sun sparkled off the metal, he inquired, 'Will this be sufficient?'

"The Indian remained stoic. Again Father reached into his pocket and this time he counted out several coins and held them in the palm of his hand for the Indian to see.

"He told the Indian, 'This is much money. Will you guide me now?'

"The Indian shook his head side to side and finally said, 'No want white man money.'

"'Then what would you take to guide me?' queried Father.

"'Take shirt you wear,' the Indian stated.

"So Father doffed his shirt, buttoned his English waistcoat tight and they were on their way, both satisfied with the deal.

"As far as Indians were concerned they did not seem to appreciate the value of the white man's money. They were far more interested in practical things."

PIONEER LIFE

"I was a pioneer to the Oregon Country and I can tell what life was like for us," related Flora Engle.

"Roads were little more than trails through the woods and transportation was by foot, horseback or by means of big farm wagons, some of these being the prairie schooners in which the settlers had crossed the plains.

"Sundays were set aside for visiting out. The entire family would climb into the wagon and bump over the rough roads to a neighbor perhaps six or seven miles away. Hospitality was unbounded and every person was the close friend and comrade of his neighbor.

"Another popular activity was picnics. Lunches would be taken, games would be played and the forest would ring with shouts of good-natured fun. How they would eat — those stalwart men! They had good times in spite of their hardships and they were happy and healthy.

"The people of our area were like one large family. What was of interest to one was of an equal interest to all. The afflictions of one household became a common cause of sorrow and the good fortune of a neighbor brought rejoicing to all.

"On those occasions when people gathered together there would be music and everybody danced from gray-haired men to the youngest girl. Other forms of group entertainment were virtually unknown.

"Very few personal conflicts marred the pioneers' lives, and always they were settled satisfactorily. And then in the 1890s a lawyer came to the settlement where I lived. Litigation through the courts became a popular pastime. It was remarked that if no lawyer had settled among us, disputes would have continued to have been mediated between neighbors with a minimum of ill feeling and at far less expense."

UNUSUAL PET

"I am from pioneering stock," Mrs. Charles Olson said. "My father, Benjamin Barlow, crossed the plains and settled on a donation land claim on the lower Columbia River.

"As a child I remember Father setting out nets to catch salmon. There were so very many salmon in those days. Father made his own nets. He kept the oak-wood needles and the material in a box nailed to the wall near the fireplace and on long evenings he worked at making nets. I would thread the needles for him.

"I also helped him make bullets. He would melt lead over red-hot coals and pour the liquid into bullet molds. He used the bullets to fire at seals, of which the river seemed to be full at times. He would shoot as many as he could but it never seemed to make much of a dent in the seal population.

"One day while Father was running the nets he found a tiny baby seal. He put it in his boat and brought it back to show us children. We, of course, begged to keep it so Father filled Mother's washtub with water, made a pen around it and we put the little seal in there. It whimpered and cried like a lost puppy. We petted and cuddled it and at first fed it milk, but as it grew older we fed it fish.

"The seal was soon too large for the washtub and could escape from its pen whenever it had a mind to. We brought it in the house where it flopped and flipped from one room to the next.

"Father said we must turn it loose and we tried, putting it in the river. But it climbed out, crawled up the bank and beat us back to the house.

"At last Father took matters into his own hands. We watched from the hill as he loaded the seal in his boat. He rowed downriver and released it. And that was the last we ever saw of our unusual pet."

RED-HAIRED BABY

Loren Brown Hastings was a school teacher living in Illinois but he had a special interest in the far west and the frontier life. When he married he promised his wife that someday they would go west.

The first child born to the Hastings, a red-haired boy, was given the name Oregon. When he was a few months old the Hastings loaded their belongings in an ox-drawn prairie schooner and departed Illinois. After six long months of travel and enduring many hardships, they arrived at The Dalles, Oregon. In later years one of Loren's favorite stories was of an experience that occurred at The Dalles.

"One day we were visited by an Indian, his squaw and their daughter, a girl of maybe 13 or 14 years old.

"My wife was holding our baby in her arms. The girl was greatly attracted to him. She oohed and ahhed about his red hair and asked if she could touch it. I allowed her to do so. And then she begged to hold the child. This, too, I allowed.

"The Indians remained all day. As they were about to depart my wife gave each of them a few small trinkets. The young maid asked if she could hold the baby one more time.

"'He is sleeping,' I informed her. She asked if she could at least see him. This I granted. She went to the wagon and I watched as she used her finger to measure his tiny feet.

"The following day the Indians returned. Again the girl asked to see our boy. He was given to her. She held him in one arm, and used the other hand to withdraw from her dress a pair of very fine buckskin moccasins trimmed with beads. These she lovingly fit on his bare feet.

"We departed from The Dalles without again seeing the Indian family. But from that single act of kindness, performed by that maiden, I can attest that even today there would never have been trouble between the Indians and the whites if only we had treated them like family."

MEDICINE DANCE

"As a young child growing up along the lower Columbia River, I well remember the Indians' medicine dances," related Thomas Strong. "Even though we were white children we were always welcome to join in.

"The sufferer would be brought into the lodge, placed upon a mat and covered with furs. At a given signal those in attendance would begin to dance, slowly at first but soon everyone would be jumping up and down and loudly chanting. Each dancer held a pole which would be thrust up and brought into contact with the roof of cedar boards in perfect time with the chanting and the jumping.

"The noise was deafening and the lodge would shake in every timber. This part of the ceremony was supposed to prepare the patient and alarm the evil spirit that had taken up residence in his body.

"All of a sudden there would be a terrific noise outside the lodge and then the medicine man and his assistants would bound through the doorway into the smoky interior with howls and yells. Their bodies were naked, their faces covered with hideous masks over which towered frightful headdresses, and in their hands were rattles, large, cumbersome things, decorated with teeth and feathers. The idea was to frighten away the demons.

"The medicine man circled with great leaps and bounds, howling like a wild animal as he went. Finally his chance would come. The spirit, which was invisible to all except the medicine man, would be caught off guard. The medicine man would rush in, seize the sick man and attempt to drag away the demon. The patient was tossed about rather roughly because Indian devils are reluctant to leave.

"In the end either the demon or the medicine man would win. If the medicine man had the stronger power the patient lived and if the demon proved stronger the patient died."

PIONEER CHILD

"I well remember crossing the plains," recalled Mrs. E.A. Hunt.

"It was in 1850. There were four of us children, Mother and Father. We had a tough go. One by one our oxen died. When we were down to a single ox Father talked to a man, Mr. Tinsley, who also had but one ox, and they agreed to go into partnership. They hitched the two oxen to our wagon, it was the better wagon, abandoned most everything except for provisions, and we continued on.

"We arrived in the Willamette Valley of Oregon late that fall. One of the oxen died so all Father had was half interest in one ox and the wagon. We settled downriver from the settlement of Portland on the Columbia slough. Father took a job splitting rails. He worked a day, maybe two, when he made a mislick with his axe and cut off all his toes on one foot. He nearly died from loss of blood, but pulled through.

"Even though I was only seven years old I had to help earn money for the family. A neighbor woman who was sick had me come in and do housework for her.

"When Father could hobble around on his lame foot he went to Portland and took a job rowing a dugout canoe, ferrying passengers back and forth across the Willamette River. Later, when the first ferryboat was built, Father ran it.

"The fall of 1851 we moved a few miles east of town, to the west slope of Mount Tabor. Father would work all week on the ferryboat and come Saturday night he would hike through the forest to our cabin and stay 'til Sunday night.

"Living like that, without a father all week, was not easy. The thing I remember most was the way the wolves would come around at night and howl outside our door. And the cougars would scream. That was terrifying for us children."

SHORT SKIRTS

Three-quarters of a century after Nancy Jane Messer had crossed the plains in a covered wagon she told an Oregon newspaper reporter, "People ask me if we had a hard time on the Oregon Trail and I tell them I never had a more enjoyable summer.

"I am old now. I speak my mind. Don't suppose you could tell by looking, but when I was young I was a mighty pretty girl. All the fellows used to brag about me, saying I had a come-hither eye. I suppose I did.

"When I was a youngster we were taught to spin and weave, make candles and soap, cook over the fire, nurse the sick and take care of children — to be good homemakers. We worked. We never had spare time on our hands.

"As I see it, the difference between the girls of my day and the modern girl is that we were taught practical things and we were also taught to be ashamed we had legs. A dress from my day, with its long train, would make a dozen dresses for wear today.

"I feel a little sorry for the contemporary woman. The poor things don't know any better. How they do like to show their calves. You would think they were prize animals at the stock show.

"I like short skirts — that is, up to my shoe-tops. But when the skirts get so short they almost disappear I think fashion has gone too far. To tell the truth, I'm afraid the girls of today are more interested in short skirts and silk stockings than in their soul's salvation. Movies and hip flasks, lipsticks and joyrides have crowded sidesaddles and camp meetings clear out of existence.

"Most of those from my era were good girls but I look at these flappers of the modern generation and wonder if they will make good wives and mothers and if they will bring up their children to be God-fearing useful citizens. Short skirts — my, my my...."

39

THE DUGOUT

The pioneering Stewart family settled on a donation land claim along the banks of the Willamette River. To get back and forth across the river Mr. Stewart hacked out a log and made a dugout canoe of it.

The spring of 1847 the river was very high and one evening at dusk a man mounted on a mule called from the opposite side, asking for someone to come get him.

Mary Stewart stepped to the front porch and shouted back, "The menfolks are gone. River's too high."

He called back, "My wife is alone. I promised her I would be home tonight. If I don't come, she'll worry."

Mary went to the dugout, pushed off into the current and, paddling furiously, was able to reach the far side. Here the man took up the paddle and directed Mary to sit in the stern and hold the mule's lead rope.

Mary related what happened next. "When we got into deep water that darn mule got scared and tried to climb into the dugout. I hit him on the head with the steering oar. He went under. The man yelled at me, 'Woman, look at what you have done! You have killed my mule!'

"I replied, 'Better to kill your mule than to have him drown the both of us.' Those words were no sooner out of my mouth than up came the mule puffing and snorting. All I had to do was to hold up the paddle in a threatening gesture and he pulled back on his lead rope.

"The man was not as good at handling the dugout as I was, so we landed quite a distance below and had to pull the boat upstream. When the dugout was secure the man reached into his trouser pocket and pulled out a $5 gold piece, saying, 'This will pay you handsomely for the risk you took.'

"His tone of voice was quite condescending and I told him, 'You keep it. I did not risk my life for a $5 gold piece. I went across and got you because I know from experience how anxious your wife must be. I did this for her.'"

THE GIRL AND THE SCALP

The Collins family came west and took a donation land claim on what had been a traditional camping ground for the Indians.

Martha Collins related, "The first summer we were there an Indian family erected their tepee very near our cabin. There was a little girl my age, eight years old. At milking time we would drink from the same cup of warm milk. She was my only playmate. We loved each other like sisters.

"She was taken sick and an Indian medicine man was called in. I was allowed in the tepee while he was beating sticks and hollering, trying to drive out the evil spirit. In spite of his effort she died. The Indians took beads, broke them up and scattered them over her. After this ceremony they buried her on a hillside near our house. They shot her horse and placed it near the head of her grave and her favorite dog they killed and put at the foot of the grave.

"The following year, when her mother came back and saw me, she cried as if her heart would break. People think Indians don't have feelings but I believe they feel as deeply and love as truly as white folks.

"Later on we did have problems with some of the Indians in the territory. When the Yakima Indian War came on they wanted recruits and my brother Mark volunteered. I did not want him to go for Father had been killed in the Cayuse War and I thought our family had shown patriotism enough. But Mark felt he should go, so I did all I could to help him get ready. The day he departed he told me, 'Don't you feel bad. I'll bring you home an Indian scalp.'

"Mark went and his company got into a pretty bad fight. During the battle Mark shot an Indian but when he ran to get his scalp the other Indians tried to prevent it. Bullets hit all around him but nary a one hit him. He brought the scalp back to me. I had it for years, but the moths worked it over, the hair began shedding and so I burned it."

41

CLARNO

Andrew Clarno was living in Illinois when the Civil War broke out. He was drafted, but rather than fight he paid a substitute to take his place.

Thinking he could avoid the war he loaded his family on a ship, the *Aerial*, and they set sail for the Pacific Coast. Near Cuba the *Aerial* was attacked and damaged by a Confederate ship but managed to escape and limp south to the Isthmus of Panama. The Clarno family crossed the Isthmus and took passage on another ship bound for San Francisco. For three years the Clarnos lived in California and then started for Oregon in a covered wagon.

Andrew wanted to ranch. He looked over southern Oregon and sized up the coast before crossing over the Cascade Mountains by way of McKenzie Pass and found country to his liking along the John Day River. He took a homestead.

The Clarnos were the first white people to settle in the region. The Indians resented the newcomers and at every opportunity they would drive off the stock. Several times the plowing team consisted of an ox and a horse. But the family was determined to make a go of it and at night Andrew would tie the stock to the side of the cabin and if there were suspicious noises he would unlimber his rifle.

Eventually the Indians were pushed onto reservations and other white men came to inspect the wide-open rangeland. One day a traveler informed Andrew that he had a neighbor, another family had taken up residence twenty miles away on the flat above the John Day canyon. Andrew immediately saddled a horse and, riding directly to the new neighbor's homestead, told the man, "There is plenty of good country. Don't you think you're crowding me a little?"

But more homesteaders flooded into the country. In 1894 a post office was established and it was agreed that the growing community should forever after be known as Clarno.

WINTERING

Eighty years after crossing the plains C.C. Masiker related the details, saying, "I have no recollections of our trip, for when we started I was but two weeks old.

"But I can tell you that our wagon train was made up at Elgin, Illinois the spring of 1853 and that we had 40 wagons in the company. We traveled west, crossed the Missouri River and struck the Oregon Trail.

"Our train was hit hard by the cholera. Mother and my sister came down with it and were not expected to live but both pulled through. However, many a family in the train suffered the loss of a loved one and some families were completely wiped out. Of the 40 wagons that started the journey only six made it through as far as Salt Lake City.

"Our family and a few others decided to winter at what was known then as Box Elder, Utah, but is now known as Brigham City. A delegation was sent to secure permission from Brigham Young since he controlled all that country.

"Brigham Young said, 'I suppose your teams are badly jaded on account of the long trip. I will send out fresh teams to you. Your men can cut down trees and haul them in.

"'Put up substantial log buildings in which to live this winter. Put up twice as many cabins as you need. I will send settlers out to occupy them. Having neighbors will make it safer for you. The Indians will be less likely to bother you.

"'If you build the cabins you are welcome to stay. Come spring you must leave and I will send other settlers to occupy your cabins.'

"Father and the other men of our party were very grateful to Brigham Young. They built a dozen log cabins. And when the tithe gatherer came around, each man dutifully paid the going rate of one-tenth of all they possessed."

BETTING THE FARM

William Gray came west in 1836 as a lay member of the Whitman-Spalding missionary expedition. The following year he was sent back to the States. He returned with a bride as well as reinforcements for the Whitman Mission at Waiilatpu.

In 1842 the Grays, having grown tired of working to convert the Indians to Christianity, left the mission and established a farm along the Willamette River.

Soon wagon pioneers were flooding into the country over the Oregon Trail. One thing they all needed was foundation stock for their farms. Gray decided to bring a herd of sheep overland, sell them to his neighbors and make a fortune in the process.

He mortgaged his farm, traveled by sea to the Isthmus of Panama, crossed overland and took passage on a ship sailing for New York City. From there he traveled west to Cincinnati and finally St. Louis, purchasing quality sheep as he went.

With spring grass coming on, Gray and three herders started 400 head of sheep over the Oregon Trail. It took three months to cross 2,000 miles. Forty sheep died along the way.

At The Dalles, Oregon, rather than risk the narrow and dangerous Columbia River trail or pay for crossing the Barlow Toll Road over the Cascades, Gray chose to float his herd and purchased a 16- by 60-foot flatbottom scow.

The trip downriver went without incident until the scow was nearing shore at the end of the journey. While the men attempted to fasten a line from the scow to shore a sudden squall struck and the line was jerked from the herders' hands. They stood helplessly as the scow was driven into the current of the Columbia. White-capped waves rolled over the deck.

Instead of making a fortune, Gray lost all 360 of his remaining sheep. He could not pay off the mortgage and he also lost his farm.

THE TRADE

The spring of 1852 the Brents family loaded their belongings in a wagon and departed Pike County, Illinois. Years later Tom Brents recalled, "I was a young lad, twelve years old, but the events of our wagon trip across the plains stand out vividly in my mind.

"Near what is now the city of Lincoln, Nebraska, the Asiatic cholera broke out. In our party nearly 100 came down with the sickness and within the span of a few days the plague killed 31 of our friends and traveling companions. One entire family was wiped out with the exception of a baby. We took the baby in. Then suddenly the sickness stopped, but for weeks after we came across numerous low mounds beside the road, grim reminders that other parties had lost some of their people, too.

"We crossed the plains, made our way through South Pass, struggled across the Snake River country and limped over the Blue Mountains. It was here, on the Columbia plateau, that one of our oxen played out. Ben was his name and he was a regular pet. Pa turned him loose. I was mighty fond of Ben and made a deal with Pa, said I would stay with Ben, let him rest a while and drive him into camp.

"Ben lay down. I tried to get him up but he would not budge. It was late in the day when a band of Indians rode up and offered to trade a sack of potatoes for old Ben. I had not tasted potatoes for several months and my desire proved stronger than my regard for old Ben, particularly as I felt pretty sure he couldn't come on without several days' rest. I swapped Ben for the spuds and started walking with my booty slung over my shoulder.

"It was well after dark before the fires of our camp came into view. Ma fixed the potatoes and we sat around savoring the taste without giving much more than a passing thought to old Ben and his most certain fate."

OREGON BOUND

"I was but a little tot when we started across the plains, bound for Oregon," related Maggie Baird.

"Few wagon trains arrived with the same number of wagons they started with. Accidents happened. Folks changed their minds. But the thing that split up most wagons trains was that the men were individualists. Some wanted to travel on Sunday. Some did not. When good pasture was reached some wanted to lay over while others wished to press on. As a result a wagon train was constantly dividing and folks who thought alike traveled together.

"Our wagon was pulled by mules and we took along a spare mule in case of an emergency. We kids fairly lived on that mule. He was gentle and he had a sweet disposition, for a mule. One day, out on the plains, a storm came up. Lightning flashed and thunder boomed. During this storm the extra mule was hit by lightning and killed. How we cried at losing such a dear and valued friend!

"Perhaps his passing was meant to prepare us for what was to come because cholera soon struck our train. Several of the grown folks died. Father took charge of the children who had been left orphans.

"When someone died a grave would be dug in the middle of the road, the person would be buried there and oxen would be driven back and forth over it so Indians would not dig up the body to get the clothing.

"There was one man in our company by the name of Curey. He was a great hand to write sad songs and of the evening we would sit around the campfire and he would sing the songs he had composed during the day. He was so homesick it was pitiful.

"One day he suddenly announced, 'I would much rather be home, starving among my own people, than to live with abundance in a strange land.' He turned back. And we continued on toward the setting sun."

THE PARTY

Ninety-year-old Mary Dunn looked back a lifetime to tell about crossing the plains by covered wagon in the 1850s.

"Father had been west during the California gold rush and had traveled between the diggings and Oregon. He said the most lovely place in all the land was the foothills of the Siskiyou Mountains. And that was where we headed.

"Eventually we reached the valley where Father wanted to settle. He filed on a donation land claim and we built a log cabin. I remember the first provisions we secured came from South America by ship and were packed over the mountains to us — flour, sugar, dried fruit and coffee. It was cheaper than paying the freight from Oregon City.

"It was up to my sisters and me to milk the cows. Mother made butter which was sold at the nearby gold mines for a dollar a pound. Tending to chores morning and evening made precious little time for fun. But that summer my sisters and I were invited to the mining settlement of Yreka to attend a big dance. Aunt Louise lived there. Father said we could go to the dance and stay with Aunt Louise.

"Some young men brought saddle horses for us and we rode over the Siskiyous, arriving in Yreka at sunset. The streets were lined with miners waiting to see us. There were very few white women in the country at the time and how they did cheer at our appearance!

"For several days we stayed at Aunt Louise's and it was a continuous reception while we were in town. But all too soon it was back home, to the cows and the incessant chores.

"To this day I carry with me a small memento of that grand party because during the festivities a young jeweler pierced my ears and gave me a pair of earrings made from Yreka gold dust. I have never removed them. And that was more than 75 years ago."

ABANDONED

When Mr. White announced at the dinner table that his family was going to Oregon his young wife was not sure of the move. "But how will we pay for it? And what about the baby? Such a trip would be very difficult on her," she cried.

"Kids are tougher than you think. Every year kids go to Oregon," said her husband. "I've made arrangements to drive an outfit and they will give us board. We can't go wrong."

The White family started over the Oregon Trail and were nearly halfway when Mr. White became ill with cholera.

His employer was a heartless man. He told Polly White, "We can't afford to lay over on your husband's account."

Then Mr. White died. Again Polly approached the owner of the wagon wanting to know, "What will happen now?"

"I hired your husband to drive. If he can't hold up his end of the bargain then the deal is off," he said coldly.

"But what will I do? And what about my baby?"

"You can walk and carry your baby. Maybe some soft-hearted soul will pick you up and give you a ride," he told her and with the crack of his whip he started his oxen, leaving the woman and child in his dust.

Polly was sitting beside the trail with her baby in her arms. She was crying. A man by the name of Woodin saw her and stopped to inquire, "What seems to be the trouble, Ma'am? Why were you left behind?"

Between sobs Polly explained her abandonment and told him, "My dead husband's brother lives near Salem, Oregon. If you will take me there I am sure he will give you the money to pay for my trip."

"I'll take you to Oregon," Mr. Woodin told her. "But I'm not going to charge you. In return you can help with the cooking and do what you can around camp."

And that was how Polly White and her baby came to Oregon. Later Polly married Mr. Knifong and together they had four pairs of twins plus a number of singles.

TURNING BACK

The spring of 1852 the Oregon-bound Turner family departed from Illinois in good spirits.

At Council Bluffs they found hundreds of other pioneers gathered, waiting their turn to be ferried across the Missouri River. It took two weeks for the Turners to reach the Kansas side where a group of 120 people formed themselves into a company. By vote they chose old man Turner to be the captain with full control of their wagon train.

They started west but within a few days Grandpa Turner became sick with cholera. He was put on a bed in the wagon but soon was too sick to travel. The wagon train was forced to lay over.

One of the pioneers, W. Boatman, wrote, "Mr. Turner died and we buried him. Again we started, but were not as light-hearted as before. We just then began to realize our condition, the thought of possibly dying hundreds of miles from our relatives, those so near and dear to us, separated from our native homes and our bodies to be left on that vast desert among the wild savages where the wolves hovered around to dig up the bodies before the train could get ten miles away."

The company continued but soon one of the Turner children became sick, died and was buried. And the following day another died and was buried. Then Grandpa Turner's son, the father of the children, came down with a fever. He lived but a few days.

As the pioneers stood over his grave Grandma Turner dabbed at her tears and said, "This is more than I can bear; losing a husband, a son, two grandchildren. Without men we can go no farther."

The other wagons went westward in search of the Oregon dream. But the Turner family, the women and children, headed back the way they had come, to Illinois and home.

50

HANGING ON

According to Mrs. McMahon, when she and her husband filed on the homestead in southern Colorado all they had was "a pocketful of dreams."

Four years later their dreams turned into a nightmare. Mr. McMahon became ill and could not plant the fields. Within a few months he was dead. Mrs. McMahon vowed to keep the homestead and raise her five children there.

The family ran out of food in February and Mrs. McMahon rode horseback through a blizzard to try to borrow food from a neighbor. But the neighbor told her they had nothing to spare. She went on to the next and he generously gave her a sack of beans.

That spring and summer Mother Nature was good to the McMahon family and they had a wonderful crop of corn growing. But a week before harvest the grasshoppers arrived, moving like a wave, a wave that consumed everything in sight. After they had passed, the corn crop looked as if it had been cut with a hand scythe.

But the worst of times still lay ahead. That fall the rains never came to dampen the soil. Instead, the wind blew and it blew and blew, ripping off the topsoil, carrying it away, drying up the river.

Nothing was left. The dreams had died; the pocket was empty. Mrs. McMahon sold the animals and took her children by the hand and they walked away. They stopped at the top of the hill, looked back and tears flowed freely. But there was no returning. They hiked to town. Within a few days Mrs. McMahon found work — cleaning houses for rich people.

GOOD LUCK HORSESHOE

Before the wagon train departed from Illinois Mary Jane Washburn had taken the time to write her children's names in indelible ink on linen and sew them inside their clothing. She said it was "just in case anything bad ever happens, so folks will know who they are."

The small wagon train crossed the plains and struggled over South Pass. It was when they reached the Snake River that tragedy struck. At camp one evening Alfred Washburn instructed his 14-year-old son, "There's more grass on the opposite side. Henry, I want you to swim the stock across and let 'em graze."

The boy obeyed but the horse he was riding was not used to the swift current and floundered. Henry tried to coax him toward shallow water but when he touched ground he reared and went over backwards, pawing at the air. Henry slipped from the saddle and was struck in the head by one of the flailing hooves.

The wagon train laid over two days while the men searched the river for Henry. But they could wait no longer so Mary Jane wrote a note giving the particulars of the accident and asking anyone who found Henry's body to please notify her family in the Willamette Valley. She posted it on a juniper tree beside the Oregon Trail.

The following year she received a letter from a Mr. Llewellyn who had settled on a donation land claim near Salem, Oregon. He wrote that he had found Henry's body and had buried him. He enclosed Henry's clothes label as well as a small horseshoe the boy had carried in his pocket. The horseshoe had been a gift from a friend and was supposed to have brought Henry nothing but good luck.

ROLLING PIN SMITH

In 1846 Jesse Applegate convinced a group of Oregon Trail pioneers to take a cut-off to the Willamette Valley of Oregon. He had blazed the new trail and promised it was easier and safer than the regular route.

But within a few days the way became much more rugged than anything they had faced. They traversed the Black Rock Desert, entered the Oregon Territory and made their way through a low pass in the heavily-timbered Cascade Mountains.

In Cow Creek canyon they were forced to cross and recross the meandering stream. Cattle slipped and fell on smooth, water-worn boulders and in their weakened condition would be content to drown rather than make the effort to get to their feet. In five days the struggling pioneers made only nine miles.

A meeting was held and the men, reasoning that even a single over-laden wagon would slow up the procession, decided everyone must lighten his load. A group went from wagon to wagon, deciding what could be kept and what must be discarded. Upon reaching the Smith family wagon, one of the men said, "Get rid of this rolling pin. It's just extra weight."

Mr. Smith was a big, rugged man. He had withstood the rigors of the trail and in times of crisis had always been a pillar of strength to the others. But now he stood quietly, staring at the rolling pin he held cradled in his arms. His eyes welled up and tears flooded out. He blubbered, "Do I have to? Do I have to throw this away? It was my mother's. I remember as a child watching her roll out the biscuits. She made such wonderful, wonderful biscuits."

The rolling pin was laid alongside the Applegate Cut-off, deep in Cow Creek canyon. And from then on Mr. Smith was addressed as Rolling Pin Smith, a nickname he endured all the rest of his days.

ROOTS

Sherwood Bonney was four years old when his father contracted pneumonia and suddenly died. When he was 12 Sherwood went his own way. He was industrious and thrifty, saved money and purchased a work team. He farmed on shares and bought land when he could. He married a neighbor girl, Elizabeth, and they began their family.

One evening Sherwood informed Elizabeth they were moving west and said they would be traveling in a wagon train that included his brother Timothy and his family.

The brothers sold their farms, purchased heavy wagons and enough supplies to last six months. They pulled out of Missouri the spring of 1852, Sherwood and Elizabeth and their six boys and Timothy and Lydia Anne and their three children.

As they traveled west an outbreak of cholera hit their wagon train. Elizabeth became ill and died. Timothy also contracted cholera and died. For the survivors there was no turning back. Sherwood and Lydia Anne combined their families and continued on.

They landed in Washington Territory and settled on a donation land claim on the north side of American Lake. The following spring they married. To this union five more children were born.

"One day," Lydia Anne related, "there arose from the back yard a loud commotion. Sherwood, quite alarmed, demanded to know the source of such noise.

"I looked out the window, smiled and told him, 'It is your children, and my children, teasing our children.'"

The Bonney family sunk their roots into Pierce County, Washington. Lydia Anne passed away in 1884 and Sherwood died at the age of 96.

MAKING A GO

"Back in 1869 I took a land claim in the Rogue River country," told P.H. Roundtree. "We had hard times and struggled just to make go of it.

"The claim was in heavy timber and brush, except for a couple acres of prairie. I built a log cabin and then, with winter coming on, the wife and I started clearing ground for a garden.

"We had more than our share of bad luck. There was quite a lot of sickness in our family. We lost four children. And stock! Stock died left and right. I don't rightly know how many head of cattle but of the first sheep I bought, six ewes, a cougar killed four in one night. Later I traded a mule for 35 head of sheep. Wolves got in and killed 28.

"Eight head of horses went down the first six years we were married. I would work around and get a nice team together and one or the other would die. I remember a time I had a good team and an Englishman came along and offered me five head of horses for my mare. It was twice what she was worth. But I would not trade. In less than three months the mare was dead.

"I traded the other horse for a yoke of oxen and used oxen for 15 years. Then I bought a cayuse for $25 and traded a cow and a calf for a mare. Right then my luck changed. I raised and sold over $2,000 worth of horses from the mare and her descendants.

"We put in a lot of sweat to make a go of the home place. The wife and I worked like a pair of beavers rebuilding a dam after a washout. The hardest of times was when the government taxed me a few dollars. Those were difficult dollars to come up with. But when they started charging me hundreds of dollars, by then money was easier to come by."

PIONEER MEMORIES

"I have resided all my life within two miles of my birthplace," said C.O. Rhodes. "Was born in the year 18 and 75 on the North Pacific coast.

"One of my earliest memories is of falling head first into a partly-filled barrel of sugar while attempting to steal a lump. Mother was outside at the time. She came in, missed me and after a search discovered my bottom side sticking from the barrel. She took full advantage of my position and instilled in me the fact I should never again steal sugar.

"When I was 12 my uncle took me fishing. This occurred in October when the salmon ascend the river from tidewater to fresh water to spawn on the gravel bars. In those days there were tens of thousands of these fish.

"Instead of a spear, my uncle used a pole with a large hook attached to the end. A cord was fastened to this hook and after snagging a fish the hook would come off the pole, in this way the pull of the fish would be on a hand-held line.

"I begged my uncle to let me hook one and, knowing full well what would happen, he handed me the pole. Not being content to stand on the bank, I crawled onto an old slippery log that projected out into the creek. Like a she bear fishing for her cubs I picked out a good, bright salmon and did I hook him! He jerked me into the water, water only maybe two feet deep and teeming with fish that were going every which way — over me, under me and all sides of me. As fast as I would gain a footing, down I would go once again with the fish bashing against me and salmon eggs in my eyes, ears, mouth.

"That was what growing up was like when I was a kid, back before the turn of the century, on the north Pacific coast."

TRAIL'S END

"I cannot hope to explain how happy our family was — Father, Mother and eight of us children — to have successfully traversed the Oregon Trail," recalled Kate Morris. "We had crossed the plains, avoided the sickness and all the mishaps that could have befallen us along the way. We had climbed over the Cascade Mountains, had tied heavy rope to the back axle of the wagon and the other end around a tree and let our wagon down Laurel Hill. We were all in good health and good spirits when we finally settled on a donation land claim in the Willamette Valley.

"We children were particularly happy, for no longer did we have to strike off each morning and walk barefooted in the dust where we stubbed our toes on rocks, stepped on prickly cactus and had to be on constant lookout for rattlesnakes. We had arrived in a country where grass for the cattle was belly-deep and when the sea breezes blew it looked like waves of green silk.

"No longer did we have to worry about the Indians running off our stock. No longer did we have to eat bacon, beans and camp bread, and not get as much of them as we wanted. We had found a country where we could have all the vegetables we wanted, where the streams were full of trout and the hills full of game.

"When we looked westward, instead of seeing a long winding train of prairie schooners with a cloud of boiling dust hanging over all, we saw vivid green fir trees and mountains. We looked up at the blue sky with white clouds, and to the east was Mount Hood, so clear and beautiful it nearly took our breath away.

"Most mornings Father would rise before sunup, follow some of the game trails and be back in time for breakfast with a deer or other wild game slung over his shoulders.

"We had landed in the Willamette Valley and truly thought we were in paradise."

Rick Steber's Tales of the Wild West Series is available in hardbound books ($12.50) and paperback books ($4.95) featuring illustrations by Don Gray, as well as in cassette tapes ($9.95) narrated by Dallas McKennon. A complete teacher study guide for the Tales of the Wild West Series is also available ($8.95). Current titles in the series include:

☐   Vol. 1   *Oregon Trail*
☐   Vol. 2   *Pacific Coast*
☐   Vol. 3   *Indians*
☐   Vol. 4   *Cowboys*
☐   Vol. 5   *Women of the West*
☐   Vol. 6   *Children's Stories*
☐   Vol. 7   *Loggers*
☐   Vol. 8   *Mountain Men*
☐   Vol. 9   *Miners*
☐   Vol. 10 *Grandpa's Stories*
☐   Vol. 11 *Pioneers*

If unavailable at retailers in your area write directly to the publisher. A catalog describing other books by Rick Steber is free upon request.

Bonanza Publishing
Box 204
Prineville, Oregon 97754